I Am The Pastor's Wife I Am

Not Perfect

Just Forgiven

Jill Howard

I Am The Pastor's Wife - I Am Not Perfect, Just Forgiven
Copyright © Jill Howard
Published By Parables

All Rights Reserved. No part of this book may be reproduced or utilized in any form or by any means, electronic or mechanical, including photocopying, recording, or by any information storage and retrieval system, without permission in writing from the author.

Unless otherwise specified Scripture quotations are taken from the authorized version of the King James Bible.

First Edition   September,, 2016

ISBN 978-1-945698-04-0

Printed in the United States of America

Readers should be aware that Internet Web sites offered as citations and/or sources for further information may have been changed or disappeared between the time this was written and when it is read.

Illustration provided by www.unsplash.com

I Am The Pastor's Wife
I Am
Not Perfect
Just Forgiven

Jill Howard

INTRODUCTION

Let me introduce myself, my name is Jill Howard and I am a Saint. No really I am! A saint is a person that is sanctified. Every born-again believer in the Lord Jesus Christ is a saint. In addition to that I am a preacher's wife and I have an opinion about everything, also I am also a mom and a mawmaw.

I was given the idea to put together this little book when I was disappointed over a bowl of cheese dip which you will read about in these pages and the Lord just kept given me ideas for other stories or articles whatever you would like to call them. Then someone said you should write a book. So here it is!

I am not perfect just forgiven. Ephesians 1:7 says "In whom we have redemption through his blood, the forgiveness of sins, according to the riches of his grace;

At the time of this printing Larry and I are members and serve the Lord at East Richwoods MBC in Mt View Arkansas where my sweet hubby is Pastor. I pray that something within these pages will tug on your heart strings because I have enjoyed putting these thoughts on paper.
Love in Christ
Jill

WHAT! NO CHEESE DIP?

I have enjoyed church fellowships all of my life. It is no different since I am grown and a preacher's wife. If your association is like ours, we have different meetings during the week; there is always something going on like youth rallies and district ladies' and men's meetings. In order to have time to get to these meetings, you and your husband probably skip supper. Always at our meetings there are just certain things you expect to be at the fellowship meal afterwards, like tuna fish salad, pimento cheese sandwiches, many different desserts, chips, cheese dip, and cold iced tea. You know they will be there and it gives you comfort knowing what to expect. After one such meeting, with all the hugs passed out and everyone caught up on everyone else's grandchildren's activities, we finally made our way back to the fellowship hall. One can only imagine my surprise (I skipped supper, came to the meeting, began getting hungry about half way through the service, and was really looking forward to getting back to the fellowship hall) as I started fixing my plate, THERE WAS NO CHEESE DIP. My heart sank. Then I made my way over the drink table and there was no tea. However, that is another story.

I took my plate and my soda over to a table and sat down. Looking at my tuna fish sandwich, my double chocolate cupcake, and the pile of chips—minus the cheese dip, I was feeling pretty disappointed. I looked at the void on my plate and thought to myself—no tea, no cheese dip! Do these people not understand tradition? Where is my comfort food? I needed it.

After the fellowship we said our goodbyes and went home. Something was wrong. I was still hungry. I lay in bed and started talking to the Lord, telling Him about the injustice of the whole meal I had experienced, and finally I drifted off to sleep. The next morning I awoke and started thinking WOW, what an AWESOME GOD we serve.

I know what to expect from Him because

the Lord is always with me and He never leaves me. His Word in Hebrews 13:5 tell me, "I will never leave thee nor forsake thee." I do not need to get comfort from food. I get my comfort from God. In John 14:18 God also tells me, "I will not leave you comfortless; I will come to you." Why am I worried about disappointments and having a void in my life? I find joy in Christ. "Verily, verily I say unto you, That ye shall weep and lament but the world shall rejoice; and ye shall be sorrowful, but your sorrow shall be turned into joy" (John 16:20).

I do not need cheese dip. I have an inheritance and reward waiting for me in heaven. "And now, brethren, I commend you to God, and to the Word of His grace which is able to build you up and give you an inheritance among all them which are sanctified" (Acts 20:32).

My God is faithful. "Let us hold fast to the profession of our faith without wavering" (Hebrews 10:23). He promises to be faithful.

I am learning God's promises in my daily walk with Him. I know not to lay up my treasures in things of this world, but in where I am going. "For where your treasure is there will your heart be also" (Matthew 6:21).

JILL HOWARD

I wonder if there will be cheese dip and iced tea in heaven—but does it really matter?

ARE YOUR PAGES FALLING OUT

Larry and I getting married is the product of a blind date and never a day goes by, before my head hits the pillow at night, that I don't I thank the Lord for sending him into my life. We were set up to meet at church; I highly recommend this if you are looking for a spouse, because this is better than any online dating site. (Some dating sites may be OK, but I don't suppose they were around when Larry and I were single.) On the Sunday we were to meet the weather was bad—in Arkansas it doesn't snow, it gets icy—and at the time I did not realize that my now sweet hubby had braved the road conditions on Saturday night to get back home from his sister's wedding—which was over 100 miles away—just to meet me. How special is that? Well, I hate to say it but I stood him up. I tell people it was just a test to see if he was a good Christian, but the truth is I just didn't want to get out on the icy roads. To my surprise he called me later that week to ask me out, so we played it safe and went to eat breakfast. That breakfast date turned into another date and we did go to church on that Sunday. I remember telling my mother that he was a good Christian man. My dear sweet saint of a mother needed more convincing. I will never forget her words of wisdom. She explained it to me this way. "When you get to church just notice his Bible. If it is a shiny new one, he is not telling you the truth, because if he is the good Christian man they are telling you he is his Bible will be worn out. I remember when we arrived at the church I looked at his Bible and the cover did look worn, so I thought to myself, this is good. When it came time for the preaching hour he picked up his Bible and the whole Book of Psalms went flying across the pew and landed on the floor.

Larry has worn out at least one Bible every year and I have kept every one of them. Each Bible has notes written in the margins and inside the covers which represents hours and hours of study. I think about the testimony that he will leave behind when the grandkids get his old worn out Bibles after the good Lord calls us home. I wonder if they will think about the hours of study each one represents. I am thankful for his testimony. My mother was one smart cookie.

In Luke 6:44-45 we read, "For a good tree bringeth not forth corrupt fruit; neither doth a corrupt tree bring forth good fruit. For every tree is known by his own fruit. For of thorns men do not gather figs, nor of a bramble bush gather they grapes. A good man out of the good treasure of his heart bringeth forth that which is good; and an evil man out of the evil treasure of his heart bringeth forth that which is evil: for out of the abundance of the heart his mouth speaketh." We are known by the fruits we produce.

Every day people watch us to see how we act or what we say. Do we want them to view us as a new shiny Bible or will people see our pages falling out?

JILL HOWARD

IT;S OK FOR MY GIRAFFE TO BE PURPLE

I recently attended a conference and we had a really great speaker who said something that struck a chord. He said "the things that happen in our lives between the age of two and twelve shape what kind of adults we become."

I have some very vivid memories from childhood. So vivid that I can remember every detail, even though sometimes I can't remember what I had for breakfast the day before. I like to think I have it all together, but on the inside I am a very insecure person. When I was a child and attended elementary school we went on field trips to the zoo. During the week before we were to go the teacher would hand out coloring sheets of different animals for us to color. We were going to make a book out of these pages to remember our trip. My coloring page was a giraffe, and I colored the giraffe purple. As I was finishing my coloring the teacher walked by and snatched up my paper and in front of the whole class she said it was stupid and that giraffe's are not purple. She then threw my paper away. I remember this like it happened an hour ago and I was so ashamed. I never told my parents and have kept this bottled up inside for most of my life, so I guess this is kind of therapy for me. Now, I am not saying that this experience shaped the adult I have become, but I feel it has played a part in my insecurity.

One thing I know for certain. My Lord and Savior loved me so much that He gave His life for me. John 3:16: "For God so loved the world, that he gave his only begotten Son, that whosoever believeth in him should not perish but have everlasting life."

Jesus gave his life for me and the color of my giraffe does not matter. He did not throw me away. Jesus is with me all the time. He lives in my heart and He will never leave me. "Let conversation be without covetousness; and be content with such things as ye have: for he hath said, I will never leave thee, nor forsake thee" (Hebrews 13:5).

I have forgiven this teacher for what she did. I'm not even sure she knew how much she was affecting my life. Adults like to believe that teachers are a positive influence in our children's lives, but I will tell you from experience -- that year was the most miserable year I spent in all my school years.

The Lord forgives us when we have sin in our life. All we have to do is ask. "If we confess our sins, he is faithful and just to forgive us our sins, and to cleanse us from all unrighteousness" (I John 1:9).

So, today I have a purple giraffe and it is the most beautiful thing in the world. Thank you Jesus!

TOOT YOUR OWN HORN

One morning I dragged myself to the coffee pot, poured myself a cup, and went to sit in my comfortable chair. Just to set the record straight, I am not a morning person. Larry was up and he wanted to share some wildlife wisdom with me, so as I stared over my coffee cup he began telling me about the whippoorwills that were calling outside. He said it was the male birds that make the musical calls to attract the females. At this time of the morning I was not amused, so I thought to myself! "That is just like a man; tooting his own horn."

I was thinking about the fact that the Lord made birds, nature, and everything around us, and we see Him in it all. And then I started thinking about God's Grace and how He extended it to me and to everyone who believes.

Some people have wrongly interpreted the Scriptures and they believe they have to work for their salvation; tooting their own horn in order to get to heaven. This must be exhausting—constantly wondering, "Did I do enough good works today to be counted worthy?" The truth is no one would ever able to do enough good works to get them into heaven. Isaiah 64:6 tells us, "But we are all as an unclean thing, and all our righteousnesses are as filthy rags; and we all do fade as a leaf; and our iniquities, like the wind, have taken us away."

Salvation is by Grace, "Not by works of righteousness which we have done, but according to his mercy he saved us, by the washing of regeneration, and renewing of the Holy Ghost; Which he shed on us abundantly through Jesus Christ our Savior; That being justified by his grace, we should be made heirs according to the hope of eternal life" (Titus 3:5-7).

Thank God we can be secure in our Salvation. Paul tells us in Romans 8:38-39, "For I am persuaded, that neither death, nor life, nor angels, nor principalities, nor powers, nor things present, nor things to come, Nor

height, nor depth, nor any other creature, shall be able to separate us from the love of God, which is in Christ Jesus our Lord."
So, I will listen to the musical calls of the whippoorwills and remember that my Savior loves me and will never leave me. What an Awesome God we Serve.

JILL HOWARD

JUST BECAUSE YOU CAN'T SEE IT DOESN'T MEAN IT'S NOT THERE

Larry has made our yard a show place, what can I say it is beautiful. He has planted flowers, trees, built buildings and a deck. We have the only chicken house with a covered front porch that the dogs and cats can lay on. Last summer he poured a concrete pad by one of the trees to put a bench and two lawn chairs on and I have to say he had some help with it. The pad was smooth and flat, just perfect with no cracks to be seen. My sister Debbie and I went to town and left him two of our granddaughters and his brother was down for a visit and when we got back home my granddaughters were just working under that tree and neither Larry nor his brother were anyhere to be seen. They were so excited when they showed me how pretty they had made the concrete pad, and there was not a smooth spot to be seen. We went in the house and Larry was kicked back in a chair and his brother was laid out on the couch, I ask Larry where the girls were and he said "Oh they are outside playing". My sister said yeah we know you should see your concrete. Larry shot up out of that chair like he was on fire and out the door he went and I was right on his heels.

As Larry was standing looking down at the concrete he held his composure and his temper, he walked over and picked up the tool that he used to smooth it out and knelt down and started working on smoothing it out again. Well the girls got upset and told him he was ruining it and he explained that he would fix them a place on the corner to decorate, both girls continued to help him so he decided to distract them with popsicles and candy so he could fix his concrete because it was getting hard to work with.

Well that lasted about three minutes and while Larry had his back turned they quickly stuck the popsicle sticks, candy wrappers plus some rocks deep down into the concrete and covered it up and stood there with big smiles because paw paw did not know what they had done. Larry finished up the concrete and as promised he let them decorate the corner. I love that corner of the concrete pad. I can just imagine one day when Larry and I have passed from this world, the girls telling their children, do you see that concrete pad? I helped my paw paw build that and there are popsicle sticks, candy wrappers and some sticks stuck way down deep in this corner under our names and foot and hand prints. There is also a recorded history of the events that happened that day, written by their maw maw.

Other than the stories my granddaughters tell about this or the recorded events of this day that I have written, would anyone have reason not to believe that there were the popsicle sticks and candy wrappers stuck safely down deep in the concrete never to be resurrected again?

I cannot physically see my Heavenly Father and I can't audibly hear Him but I know he is there. I talk with my Father just like I talk with a friend that is sitting right beside me, but I can't see him and I can't hear him talk back to me. I can't reach out and touch Him. So how can I have a relationship with someone I can't see, touch or carry on a conversation with? How do I know he is there? I know He is there by Faith "Now faith is the substance of things hoped for, the evidence of things not seen" Hebrews 11:1 and I can read the events that are recorded in the inspired Word of God. The Bible is perfect and complete "All scripture is given by inspiration of God, and is profitable for doctrine, for reproof, for correction, for instruction in righteousness" II Timothy 3:16. I can find answers to any questions I have had, that I have or ever will have. I can read about creation in Genesis chapter 1, to Jesus' birth, ministry while he was on earth, His death, burial and resurrection found in Matthew, Luke and John in the New Testament.

The Lord speaks with me through His written Word; I can talk with him in prayer and be watchful for his answers. "If ye abide in me, and my words abide in you, ye shall ask what ye will, and it shall be done unto you" John 15:7. I have a relationship with my Heavenly Father because I believe He sent His Son to die for my Sins, "For God so loved the world, that he gave his only begotten Son, that whosoever believeth in him should not perish, but have everlasting life" John 3:16. I have confessed my Sins to my Father and ask Him to come into my heart.

He saved me because I asked Him too, I believe His Holy Word.

Oh I almost forgot, the next morning when Larry went out to check his concrete there were little paw prints across it where the dog wanted to make it pretty.

When God Calls Don't Let It Go To Voicemail!

Last week I was having a really stressful day at work; if one thing went wrong twenty others followed close behind. I remember saying a little prayer. "Ok, Lord, my plate is full!" Right then I heard my phone ring. It was my husband's ringtone so, I just let it ring. I had too much other stuff going on and I did not have time to stop. I heard the voicemail tone so I told myself I will check it later. After a while I did check my message and the voice of our four-year-old granddaughter was on the recording saying, "Mawmaw hello, hello, HELLO, HELLO!"

I returned the call and my husband gave the phone to our granddaughter. She started telling me that she was at my house with her Pawpaw and they had watched cartoons, ate pink ice-cream, petted the dog, and put his sweater on him (I bet he loved that). She went on telling me some stuff I could not understand, but I acted excited and let her know that what she had to say was very important to me; and it was. When she was finished she said bye and hung up. The rest of my day was stress-free and uneventful.

That night I was thanking God for all His blessings and His watch care over my family. I remembered that earlier that day everything was hectic -- but after my phone call from my granddaughter my focus had changed -- and all of the stressful feelings disappeared. Remembering this I began to wonder. Lord, do I let your message go to voicemail? I am afraid I do. Sometimes I just get so hung up in all the stuff that goes on that I put my prayer life on the back burner; forgetting to talk to my Heavenly Father; and that's when things tend to get out of control because I have lost my focus.

God communicates with us through prayer and the reading and studying of His Word. He instructs us in 1 Thessalonians 5:17 to "Pray without ceasing" and in 2 Timothy 3:16 we are told, "All Scripture is given by inspiration of God, and is profitable for doctrine, for reproof, for correction, for instruction in righteousness," so therefore we must heed 2 Timothy 2:15 and "Study to shew thyself approved unto God, a workman that needeth not to be ashamed, rightly dividing the Word of truth."

God wants us to have a constant, consistent prayer life. In Philippians 4:6 we read, "Be careful for nothing; but in everything by prayer and supplication with thanksgiving let your requests be made known unto God." When we are having stressful days let us remember what He tells us in Philippians 4:13. "I can do all things through Christ which strengtheneth me."

I know when I pray to my Heaven Father He hears me the first time. He does not have to get back to me at a later time. I know that what I have to say is important and the Lord wants to hear about it, no matter if I am just telling Him I ate some pink ice-cream, or that I have a problem and I need Him to show me some direction so that His Will is done and not mine.

I am truly thankful that the Lord does not have voicemail.

JILL HOWARD

THE PROTECTION OF A CHICKEN

I came home from work and my husband Larry was outside and told me he wanted to show me something. We walked out to the chicken pen and there was a fuzzy black chick with two hens taking care of him. It was funny watching the two hens clucking, calling to the chick and protecting it. The next morning Larry said the two hens were side by side with the little fellow sitting on top of them. I don't think we have to worry about anything happening to this chick. Our little hens make good mothers nurturing and teaching their little ones the ropes and I am sure that either one of them would give their life to protect their little chick from the dangers that are around every corner, that is a mother's love.

This reminded me of the story in 1 Kings 3:16-28 of the two women who claimed the same child and went to the wise King Solomon to settle the dispute. The story goes on to say that the king told one of his men to take a sword and cut the child in half and give each woman half. The real mother started pleading not to harm the child and give it to the other woman. King Solomon could see the love the woman had for the child and knew she was the real mother.

Just as the love of a parent has for a child my Heavenly Father loves me. In Romans 8:39 it says "Nor height, nor depth, nor any other creature, shall be able to separate us from the love of God, which is in Christ Jesus our Lord."

The Lord protects his children just as the shepherd protects his sheep. John 10:10-11 "The thief cometh not, but for to steal, and to kill, and to destroy: I am come that they might have life, and that they might have it more abundantly. I am the good shepherd: the good shepherd giveth his life for his sheep".

If we will just open our eyes and look around we will see examples of God's love, even in the chicken pen.

ARE YOUR GARMENTS SPOTLESS?

Early in my husband Larry's ministry someone told him, "A preacher should look like a preacher" and the best we can figure out is that it means a coat and tie, since that was the only two articles of clothing he had removed between the morning and the evening service. I tend to agree with this person, but I believe it should apply, not only to the preacher but, to every Christian. Matthew 18:20 tells us, "For where two or three are gathered together in my name, there am I in the midst of them." I just feel that if Jesus is in our midst we should look our best. (Don't shoot me; I am just weird that way.)

On Saturdays I spend time making sure

our Sunday best is clean, ironed, and not in need of repair, so the next morning it will go smooth when we are getting ready for worship. This does not always happen as planned. I will say that our best is not expensive, but at least it is clean most of the time. Let me explain! We get ready, give each other the once over to make sure everything looks good, then something happens between the time we get in the car and when we arrive at church. Sometimes I have looked at Larry once we get inside the church house and I have noticed a big glob of tooth paste on his tie and/or shirt, gravy on his shirt sleeve, cat hair on his coat, and recently after the service he had tooth paste in his hair. I'm still trying to figure that one out.

I tend to panic when I discover something on him because I fear some sweet saint sees the same thing and thinks to herself, "Boy that preacher's wife is not taking care of the preacher. You know in Ecclesiastes 9:8 we're told, "Let thy garments be always white; and let thy head lack no ointment." Yeah, right. Not in the Howard household. I have invested in a lint brush, a Tide Pen, and a small sewing kit that I keep in my purse. I know it's not the outside that counts, but what's on the inside. I am thankful the Lord sees us differently than we see ourselves or each other. We can't hide anything from God.

In I Peter 3:3-4 we read, "Whose adorning let it not be that outward adorning of plaiting the hair, and wearing of gold, or of putting on of apparel; But let it be the hidden man of the heart, in that which is not corruptible, even the ornament of a meek and quiet spirit, which is in the sight of God of great price."

As long as we live here in our earthly body we will always have cat hair on our coat, but I know I have the Robe of Righteousness spoken of in Isaiah 61:10. "I will greatly rejoice in the Lord, my soul shall be joyful in my God; for he hath clothed me with the garments of Salvation, he hath covered me with the robe of righteousness, as a bridegroom decketh himself with ornaments, and as a bride adorneth herself with her jewels."

WAITING AT THE END OF THE DRIVEWAY

When I travel to and from work sometimes I leave the house about the time the school bus runs. I have noticed a little boy standing at the end of his driveway waiting on the bus and he has a big brown dog that is always standing with him. On more than one occasion I have driven by that house after the bus had run and that big old dog was laying at the end of the driveway looking like he had lost his best friend. I have often thought to myself I wonder if that dog waits there all day.

One afternoon I was behind the bus and it stopped at that house and the dog was wagging his tail waiting for his master to get off the bus. I could not help but smile when I saw the reunion between the boy and his dog as they ran happily towards the house. I began thinking about the Prodigal Son that we read about in the book of Luke 15:11-32. The Son wanted his share of his inheritance and he didn't want to wait. He spent it and found himself eating with the pigs so he decided to go home to be a servant in his father's house. But when his father saw him what happened? The father welcomed him with open arms, no questions ask. Luke 15:20 reads: "And he arose, and came to his father. But when he was yet a great way off, his father saw him, and had compassion, and ran, and fell on his neck, and kissed him. What a happy reunion!

I am a sinner and sometimes (more than I care to count) I stray from the protection of my Father's loving arms. I let the world influence me and before I know it I might have forgotten to pray or open God's Word to see what he has for me. Now notice I said I am the one who strays, God never leaves me. We read in 1 John 1:9; "If we confess our sins, he is faithful and just to forgive us our sins, and to cleanse us from all unrighteousness." It is a comfort to know that when I do repent and run back to my Father, He is waiting on me with open arms.

NO MILK JUGS REQUIRED

Larry came in the house last week and announced that he had his first tomato on his vines. He tries to have a vegetable garden every year but to be honest he is better at growing flowers than vegetables. My not-so-green-thumbed hubby planted these tomato plants and then the weather turned cold. Only in Arkansas can you have freeze warnings in the middle of April. Anyway, He cut the bottom out of milk jugs to cover and protect them from the elements. I was watching him from the window and you know by now how my mind works, so when he came in I waited for him to get settled and I went in and said "Larry, you are so brilliant, I did not know you planted milk plants and it looks like they are ready for harvest." Now who doesn't see the humor in that?

I feel much safer knowing God has His hand of protection over me and I do not have to rely on man-made objects. However I am thankful for seat belts; just saying. The Lord prepares us for the battles we face every day when we read His Word and spend time in prayer with our Heavenly Father. In Ephesians 6:11 we read, "Put on the whole armour of God, that ye may be able to stand against the wiles of the devil." (This is Spiritually speaking)

Last year at this time we had one tomato plant and we were patiently watching a tomato grow when one afternoon Larry looked at it and the beautiful plant was GONE. He found it wilting on the ground. A cut worm was doing his job and cut it off. It was humbling to say the least.

An example of physical protection is recorded in Daniel 6:22. "My God hath sent his angel, and hath shut the lions' mouths, that they have not hurt me forasmuch as before him innocency was found in me; and also before thee, O king, have I done no hurt." and in the last part of verse 23 it tells us that "no manner of hurt was found upon him, because he believed in his God."

While we still rely on God for protection,

at times we find ourselves in harm's way and things happen to us causing us to have to look to God for guidance, often suffering persecution and maybe even death. Look to Luke 21:12-16. Our Savior Himself tells us in Luke 21:18, "But there shall not an hair of your head perish." We will live totally whole in the Kingdom of God.

When relying on God no milk jugs are required. I can say, life with Larry is never dull and he does provide some great writing material.

FISH FOR BREAKFAST...ANYONE?

Larry and I enjoy going fishing and there is a beautiful lake close to where we live that we fish at from time to time. Just for the record Larry goes more than I do. The last couple of times we went there we noticed a playful otter and he loves to put on a show for the frequent visitors to the lake.

One morning Larry and I went fishing at this lake and were catching some fish and having a rather good time when we heard some people up the bank yelling "Here he comes", not sure what was going on we noticed some bubbles coming towards our fish stringer and then something started pulling it rather forcefully. Larry went to grab the stringer and there was the otter on the other end of the stringer with a death grip on the largest fish, so the tug a war game was on. Larry managed to get the fish away from the otter and was feeling victorious over his win and went on up the bank to another fishing spot. I was enjoying the view and listening to the water falling over the dam and thinking to myself the sounds were so peaceful…God made this! By that time about half a hour passed by and I heard some splashing and sure enough the otter was back, I called for Larry and he came running and grabbed the stringer again and this time he pulled the otter up out of the water onto the bank, Everyone was watching the battle for the fish and it was pretty funny, then the otter snapped the fish off the stringer and hopped back to the water with his breakfast. Larry surveyed the fish that was left on the stringer and they were in shreds.

It was some time later the friendly otter came back and was rolling in the water in front of us making some squeaking noises. I told Larry "Look he is doing a victory dance". In the back of my mind I was thinking this is really cute but I do not think Larry was not sharing my interpretation of humor.

We read about the temptation of Eve found in Genesis chapter 3 verse 4 "And the serpent said unto the women, Ye shall not surely die:"

Satan is the master of deception and temptation. Sometimes sin comes our way and we can resist it the first time but then Satan has a way of disguising it to look playful, cute and harmless much like that little otter and we let our guard down for just a second and it grabs hold of us and leaves our testimony in shreds much like the fish that was left on the stringer, now noticed I did not say we can lose our Salvation but I do believe we can lose the joy of our Salvation and blessings from God.

We all know that we have a sinful nature and no one wants to sin purposely, but when we do fall into Satan's net (or stringer) our Father is just to forgive us our sins.

1 John 1:9 reads "If we confess our sins, he is faithful and just to forgive us our sins, and to cleanse us from all unrighteousness." and in Chapter 2 verse 1 we read "My little children, these things write I unto you, that ye sin not, And if any man sin, we have an advocate with the Father, Jesus Christ the righteous: verse 2 reads "And he is the propitiation for our sins: and not for our's only, but also for the sins of the whole world."

God's creation is awesome (otter and all). Anyone ready to go fishing?

I WOULD RATHER HAVE THE CHEESE

I opened my Facebook page the other morning and noticed that at some point I must have joined a devotional group because there was their morning's devotion on my page: accompanied by a picture of a big blue bird with a worm in its mouth and a caption that read "The early bird gets the worm". I quickly made a comment that read "Well, the second mouse gets the cheese". Being that quick witted, especially that early in the morning, made me feel kinda proud, but I suppose the person who authored this particular devotion did not appreciate my humor (imagine that) and I was voted out of the group. Before this page vanished off of my page, never to be seen again, I started reading the devotion and discovered that it was about works for Salvation. The person that wrote this devotion was leaving Jesus out of the equation and instead living under the misconception that they could get to heaven by doing good works. Well, we as Christians know that our works do not get us to heaven. Reading in 2 Timothy 1:9 we learn, "Who hath saved us, and called us with an holy calling, not according to our works, but according to his own purpose and grace, which was given us in Christ Jesus before the world began."

Our world seems to be filled with people who are focused on selfs. Everyone is looking out for number one. It's all about ME ME ME! I know people who put themselves before their spouse and before their children. This breaks my heart. One commercial in particular that disturbs me has a woman with her feet up on a man's desk and she is saying to the man, "You should be asking me what I can do for you". This is what our children learn when they watch those big ugly boxes we have in our houses. Whatever happened to Jesus, Others, and then You?

I am so glad that Jesus loved me so much that He died on that awful cross for me and for anyone else who will accept this cheese.

Oh wait, I meant Gift. You do not have to work for it, just accept it. "For whosoever shall call upon the name of the Lord shall be saved" (Romans 10:13). However, as a result of accepting this gift, you will want to work to receive the crowns that we will give back to our Savior. "And, behold, I come quickly; and my reward is with me, to give every man according as his work shall be" (Revelation 22:12).

WOW! To think about this and what an awesome God we serve is wonderful beyond words!! So, I will just wait for the cheese, because Jesus has already paid the price and His gift is there for mankind to accept or reject. If you are reading this article and you do not know Jesus as your Personal Savior, my prayer is that you will accept Him now. Please do not wait until it is too late!

WORRY WART

Towards the end of my mother in laws life she suffered with dementia. She had been admitted to the hospital and Larry and I went to visit her. My husband asked her if she knew who I was. She looked at me and said, "Yes, I know who she is." My husband then asked her what my name was and she responded, "Worry Wart."

Just in case you do not know what a worry wart is I looked it up on the internet and it said "A worry wart is a person who is naturally nervous, living out his or her life in a state of worry". (I have to say you can find a lot of useful information on the internet as well as some useless information).

Well she was right I am a worry wart. I worry about everything. My family, my job, if I have a runner in my pantyhose, does my dress fit, did our members like the bulletin this week, was my dish for the potluck any good and this list goes on. I recently read a posting on Face Book (yes I facebook) that said "if you worry you miss out on the joys around you". I agree with that and I do miss out on a lot of things that should be a joyous event but I have worried the joy right out of it.

In Matthew 6:27 we read " Which of you by taking thought can add one cubit unto his stature?" ...OK in Jill's translation.... you can worry all you want to but it does not change the outcome. I know it is not man I have to worry about pleasing, it is my Heavenly Father that I will stand in front of one of these days and stand accounted for. But one thing I have to never worry about is the love Jesus has for me and He will always love me. "For God so loved the world, that he gave his only begotten Son, that whosoever believeth in him shall not perish, but have everlasting life". John 3:16. Jesus has and always will love me, and I am going to spend eternity with Him.

My potluck casserole may be burnt on the bottom, and if I am going to have a runner in my pantyhose it will be there if I worry or not. It is easy to say I am going to give this situation to the Lord but before I get done praying I have already taken it back and I did not give the Lord a chance to take care of it. Boy I sure can make a mess out of things. Have you ever done that?

Jesus told his disciples "Consider the ravens: for they neither sow nor reap; which neither have storehouse nor barn; and God feedeth them: how much more are ye better than the fowls?" Luke 12:22

And I have to say I have never heard of a bird with high blood pressure or stomach ulcers from worry. My husband's sermon this coming Sunday is about examples found in the Bible for our daily life. I wonder if he was reading my mind? If we would read our Bible daily and when we needed some wisdom, it has all the answers to our problems and questions and that would decrease a lot of needless worry.

I read somewhere that worry is like a rocking chair, it gives you something to do but gets you nowhere. So as Christians just turn your worries over to the Lord... it's OK... He's got this.

.

It's Time!

Since Larry has surrendered to the ministry the Lord keeps him busy filling in for different preachers. He has preached in view of a call at some places as well. We both really enjoy visiting other churches and meeting new friends and rekindling old friendships. The Lord has really blessed us. I love to watch Larry prepare for a message when he studies and spends time in prayer. I admire my husband for his boldness as he preaches the Word and the fact that he is not intimated by the clock. One thing that I have noticed in every church we visit and I have been guilty myself that there is a universal sign that when the clock gets to about 10 minutes before the hour to end you will start to hear Bibles being slammed shut and the song books being zinged out of the back of the cozy nooks on back of the pews, then just in case the preacher did not hear the first mild hints you will hear the sounds of zippers being zipped on the Bible cases. This is the sign that it is time for the service to come to a close and it is time for lunch. It's time for the Lords People to get busy the fields are ready for the harvest, it tells us in John 4:35 "Say not you, There are yet four months, and then comes harvest? behold, I say to you, Lift up your eyes, and look on the fields; for they are white already to harvest." The Great Commission found in Matthew 28:19-20 it reads " Go ye therefore, and teach all nations, baptizing them in the name of the Father, and of the Son, and of the Holy Ghost: Teaching them to observe all things whatsoever I have commanded you: and, lo, I am with you always, even unto the end of the world." It's Time! As we live our lives let's not be found guilty of slamming the Bible shut or zipping our zippers on our Bible cases only the Lord knows the day and the hour so it's time to get busy.

Please Don't Drink The Bird Food

On a warm spring afternoon as my husband and I were sitting outside enjoying the warmth of the afternoon and watching the wildlife that lives in our back yard, our granddaughter came out the back door and made the announcement that she poured her own drink and then went on to say "That Red Kool Aid is Really Sweet". At that time I realized that my granddaughter had just consumed the humming bird food that my husband keeps mixed up in the refrigerator to fill his bird feeders. I had a moment of uneasiness in the pit of my stomach as I was thinking about the effect the nectar sweet liquid would have on her kidneys, and her blood sugar.

I thought to myself "That child is not going to sleep for a week from the sugar high she is going to receive". I began to think about the world we live in today, we have things all around us that look sweet and harmless but it is disguised as something else. In our busy lives we tend to take things at face value without looking at the big picture. Today we have churches of all different sizes that look good on the outside and you would believe they are godly places of worship but instead they are a collection of man-made activities to keep us and our young ones entertained, where we come away feeling good on the outside that only last until you get to the parking lot. What is missing, you still have empty place inside that still needs to be filled with substance. You did not meet God there, he has been replaced with worldly ideas and music that appeals to the flesh and does not bring honor and glory to the One that gave His life for you and me. As Christians we must be prepared and armed with the Truth to know the difference between a worldly place and a godly place of worship. How do we do this? By prayer, study, and knowing what is in God's Word. In 1 John 4; 1, 2 it tells us "Beloved, believe not every spirit, but try the spirits whether they are of God:

Because many false prophets are gone out into the world. Verse 2 says "Hereby know ye the Spirit of God: Every spirit that confesseth that Jesus Christ is come in the flesh is of God". Then we are to "be strong in the Lord, and in the power of his might" Ephesians 6:10 and in the following verses 11-17 it tells us to put on the whole armor of God, that ye may be able to stand against the wiles of the devil.

Remember just because it looks good on the outside that does not mean it is good for you on the inside. Maybe I will put a label on the bird food in the refrigerator just in case.

WHERE'S JESUS?

In the city where I work there is a large church on the corner of a busy street, and this past Christmas season I noticed they had a nativity scene set up close to the street. I had driven by the church house many times going to work and one day I got stopped by a red light right there in front of the nativity scene and I had to take a second look because I could not believe my eyes, baby Jesus was missing and I mean the manger and all.

I arrived at work and asked, "Did you know baby Jesus was missing from the nativity scene on the corner?"

One of the ladies I work with said yes they did not put Him out this year because they did not want to offend anyone. I could not believe what I was hearing. I just have to say this "THAT OFFENDS ME."

The Bible tells us in Psalm 44:8 "In God we boast all the day long, and praise thy name forever".

As Christians we are instructed to profess Christ and if we tip toe around so we don't offend someone are we really professing Christ?

In Ephesians 6:19-20 it says "And for me, that utterance may be given unto me, that I may open my mouth boldly, to make know the mystery of the gospel. For which I am an ambassador in bonds: that therein I may speak boldly, as I ought to speak."

During the Christmas season if someone gives you a gift, what do you do with it? You happily receive it.

God gave us the most valuable gift, and all we have to do is receive it. "For God so loved the world, that he gave his only begotten Son, that whosoever believeth in him should not perish, but have everlasting life" John 3:16

This Christmas let's put Jesus back in Christmas and I don't mean just back in the nativity scene, let's put Him in our hearts and proclaim Him boldly, and let's do this every day of the year.

JILL HOWARD

NOT PERFECT, JUST FORGIVEN

JILL HOWARD

NOT PERFECT, JUST FORGIVEN

JILL HOWARD

www.ingramcontent.com/pod-product-compliance
Lightning Source LLC
Chambersburg PA
CBHW071544080526
44588CB00011B/1785